Between a Rock and a Hard Place:

Making Choices

Robin Schneider Larkin

SHIRES ♦ PRESS
4869 Main Street
P.O. Box 2200
Manchester Center, VT 05255
www.northshire.com

Between a Rock and a Hard Place: Making Choices
©2018 by **Robin Schneider Larkin**
ISBN: 978-1-60571-436-3

Building Community, One Book at a Time
A family-owned, independent bookstore in
Manchester Ctr., VT, since 1976 and Saratoga Springs, NY since 2013.
We are committed to excellence in bookselling.
The Northshire Bookstore's mission is to serve as a resource for
information, ideas, and entertainment while honoring the needs
of customers, staff, and community.

Printed in the United States of America

For my clients—I have learned so much from you.

Table of Contents

Introduction		Page 1
Chapter 1	Attitude is everything	Page 3
Chapter 2	Assertion is not the same as aggression.	Page 7
Chapter 3	Not making a decision is still making a choice.	Page 13
Chapter 4	There is no right or wrong choice.	Page 17
Chapter 5	You can. You choose not to.	Page 21
Chapter 6	Meditation	Page 25
Chapter 7	Simplify	Page 29
Chapter 8	Fine, I'll decide. But how?	Page 33
Conclusion		Page 41

Introduction

I remember a conversation with my mother about my future when I was a teenager. She said she thought it must be hard to have so many career options, and she did not know how I would choose what I wanted to be. My mother was born in 1929. When she was deciding what to do after high school, she did not have many choices. Her father told her she could only go to college if she wanted to be a nurse or teacher. She knew she didn't want either of those careers so she went to work on a factory line. She loved it. Her father, however, did not love his daughter working in a factory so he convinced her to become a secretary at an engineering company in the city. There she met my father, got married and became a housewife and mother, which she also loved.

As a young woman in the mid-1980s, I never considered the myriad of options open to me a burden. The thought of doing the same thing for forty-plus years seemed boring, so thinking I had a lot of options was a good thing. Also, my sister-in-law had shared her perspective about choosing a college major: "You don't have to be the same thing for the next forty years! You can change your mind." I took that to heart and have felt free to change my work/life choices throughout the past thirty-plus years.

Of course, not everyone has a lot of choice when it comes to their career path. For those born into a lower socioeconomic upbringing, there may be fewer choices due to financial and educational constraints. For those born into families of social or economic privilege, there may be fewer options due to family obligations. A family of doctors or athletes often puts pressure on their offspring to join the family "business." However, regardless of socio-economic status or privilege, people can reach a point in their lives where all their choices seem predestined or out of their hands.

There is no question that we all make choices every day. And that each of those choices will impact the number and quality of choices we will have access to in the future. The first lesson in learning how to make a productive choice is to understand that you have a choice. This book is a follow-up to my first book, *Stop Talking to Yourself and Start Listening,* where I encourage people to live the life they want. In the following chapters of this book, I will show you how to make choices that will not only empower you, but also, will help you create the life you envisioned when reading my first book.

Chapter 1

Attitude is everything.

Do you take advantage of the choices open to you? I recognize everyone does not have the same choices available to them. But we all have choices. We choose to react or respond to others. We choose to pursue options, or not. We choose to open up options or shut them down. Life is full of choices, and how we perceive them determines how we will respond to them.

If you have done your boundary work, choices will be more comfortable to make. When someone asks you to do something for them, do you get mad at them for asking? Then you need to work on your boundaries. Once you are comfortable setting boundaries, responding "no" to someone becomes a much easier choice. A request for help—whether it is to serve on a committee or care for a loved one—is simply a question. And you have a choice to make. If you have prioritized your time in accordance with your values, than saying yes or no will become easier. Your choice will be "Yes, I can" or "No, I can't" with no need to rationalize or explain. If this seems too difficult, see chapter five, *Boundaries*, in my previous book, *Stop Talking to Yourself and Start Listening*.

Here is an example. A friend asks you to join a committee and you make the choice to say "No, I can't." And your friend makes their own choice to take offense or get upset. Now, *you* have another choice to make. You can react emotionally like they did, or you can simply respond. Keep in mind that your "no" is not *against them*, but it is *for you*. When we respond instead of react, our positive attitude sets the tone for the conversation. A positive attitude can be established by setting healthy boundaries in your own life—and this will allow for easier decision making when choices arise.

Sometimes choices are scary or uncomfortable. A job opportunity in another state or a chance encounter with an intriguing stranger can create exciting choices. At the same time, the possibility of change brings with it some uncertainty. It can be helpful to acknowledge that the change is what is scary—not the choice. Not everyone likes change. If you are living your life according to your life plan, the choice becomes easier. Does this choice move you closer to your goals? If not, then "no" becomes the easier/better response. If it does move you closer to your goals, then talk to a trusted person in your support network about the specifics you are most concerned about.

For example, after I earned my master's degree, I went back to work for the first time in fifteen-plus years. Prior to that, I was a stay-at-home mom and part-time owner of a weaving business. Family meals were my domain. I created the menus, did the food shopping and the cooking. And I liked it that way. I can be a picky and discerning eater so being in charge of meals was a comfortable choice for me. Then, I made the decision to go back to school, and later, to work. I had gotten over my fears of the work changes, but I was stuck on the home changes. *My husband is a fine cook*, I thought, *but trust him with dinner regularly?* I wasn't looking forward to it.

OK, I get it. To you, that might sound trivial, but I was worried about how I would react when the meals didn't meet my high standards. So, I had conversations with friends who calmed my fears about this change. I remember my friend, Sue, saying, "Trust me, you are just going to be grateful he's putting food in front of you." I became comfortable with that home change because it moved me closer to my goal, and I accepted the changes that were less palatable with a positive attitude. I talked with trusted friends and I let go of some control. These smaller choices were all part of my bigger choice to re-enter the workforce.

When choices are difficult, then your attitude about them is probably negative. In this situation, it is important to recognize that the problem isn't the choice; the problem is your attitude. Change your attitude by recognizing that it's your life. Live it the way you see fit and not the way others believe you should. Create a strong support network of trusted people you can ask for help or feedback. If your network contains people who make your choices harder, you might need to change the people you ask. Create a support network of people who do support you and live their lives in a way you admire. Choose people who have strong boundaries and live their lives according to their wants and needs. This will make asking for help a more positive experience which, in turn, will make your own choices easier to manage.

Chapter 2

Assertion is not the same as aggression.

Sometimes, when making a choice, we need to stand up for ourselves. Many people will say, "I don't like being confrontational." But standing up for ourselves does not have to be done with an aggressive stance. We can assert ourselves without being aggressive. Often, people become aggressive or confrontational when they are standing up for their choices because they feel defensive about their decisions. Saying "no" or doing what *you* want—instead of what your parent, partner, friend, or co-worker wants—is a much harder road when you haven't established strong boundaries. Once you are comfortable running your life according to your own desires and specifications, asserting yourself will become easier and you will be less likely to become defensive or aggressive.

Years ago, I was having a conversation with my mother-in-law. She presented her idea that my husband and I should purchase a duplex for our first home and rent out one-half for income. I responded that I didn't want to be a landlord. She kept describing and defining the concept so that I would change my mind. I felt like she was pushing me to do something I had already said I did not want to do. Finally, I said assertively and clearly, "I am familiar with the concept of being a landlord to help pay your mortgage. I do not want to do that." I wasn't rude or confrontational. I did, however, state my intentions and thoughts clearly and succinctly. She got it and dropped the idea. She wasn't happy about it, but that is beside the point. I stood strong in my decision and was assertive in my response.

When someone presents us with a choice, we have two options. We can agree and choose "yes" or we can decline and say "no." Would you like the beef or chicken is an easy choice and not likely to create an issue. However, a discussion regarding a career choice or whether you will follow a family tradition can be more problematic. In some families, careers are predestined; maybe everyone becomes a doctor or a police officer or a career in the arts isn't valued. If your passion propels you toward a career choice that is not family-approved, the discussions about your choice may be difficult. Reminding yourself to be assertive—and not aggressive—will get you through these conversations with the least disruption. When you are assertive, you stand strong in your own beliefs: It is your life and you are free to make your own career choices.

Prior to or during one of these discussions, if you begin to get defensive, ask yourself, why? Is it because you doubt your choice or because it is frustrating when people you love don't trust you to make good decisions? Think about that question ahead of time. Do loved ones often question your ability to make good decisions? If so, is there any evidence to back up their concern? If there is no evidence to back up their lack of faith in your decision-making ability, remember what you learned from my first book, in chapter six, *Don't mind-read*, and chapter seven, *No one makes you feel anything*. Respond to your family's questions. Don't react.

It's true, we can feel frustrated. This only means you need to direct the discussion with assertiveness. Assertively explain why you are happy with your decision. Recognize that having a discussion about your choice actually might not be a good option. You could choose to simply inform rather than discuss.

Prior to or during the discussion, if you realize you are unsure of your decision, the discussion will go in a different direction—one where you are looking for advice and guidance on the choice. If, during the discussion, you realize you need different people—perhaps outside the family—to help you, assertively extricate yourself. Say something like:

"Thank you for your thoughts and concerns. You have given me some things to think about."

This allows you to exit the discussion without agreeing or disagreeing. At the end of each day, you are the one living your life and, therefore, you should be the one to decide. However, if your decision affects others, like partners or children, you need to include them in the decision-making process.

Choices that do affect others like partners or children still need to be handled assertively, not aggressively. When we are assertive, we speak in clear voices without trepidation. We do not raise our voices or name call. We do not get emotional or attack. We focus on the hows and whys of our choice. We listen to the concerns of partners and family members and address them with consideration. These are important people in our lives and we need to value them.

Respect and consideration are a two-way street. For example, when parents choose to sell the family home there may be dismay, anger, or tears by grown children who no longer live in the home but have strong connections to it. For the parents, assertively discussing the choice to sell means explaining how the house no longer fits their needs and how life will change once the house is sold. A smaller house may or may not continue to allow for large family gatherings like big Thanksgiving dinners. Recognizing the changes a choice will create means everyone's thoughts and feelings on the subject are valued. For the children in this scenario, talking about the changes in a positive way can take time. Feelings on the subject must be honored. This does not mean you have the authority to change another person's decision. In this example, while it may be emotionally difficult to see the family home sold the parents should not continue to live in a house that doesn't fit their needs anymore.

The same type of discussion is needed when a choice involves a partner. If you are sharing a life with someone, much of what you do affects that person. Hating your well-paying job means you are unhappy and seriously stressed. That affects your partner. Taking a more enjoyable job that pays a lot less will improve the emotional environment of your shared space. However, the smaller paycheck will also affect that same environment. Respect those changes when you are assertively discussing this choice with your partner. Again, don't mind-read or fall for the idea that they can "make" you feel a particular way. Your choice affects them and they are entitled to have feelings about it. Stand strong in your strength and assertively discuss your choice to change jobs. When resolving disagreements over choices that affect the lives of two or more people—such as parents and children—mutual respect and clear, concise explanations will go a long way to a peaceful and satisfying conclusion.

During discussions about your choice, note when you are beginning to get emotional, defensive, or aggressive. If this happens, take a deep breath and a step back. Being assertive means standing strong on your life's path. Respond to others and work to not react emotionally even when the other person becomes emotionally reactive. Continue to set a mutually respectful tone for the conversation. When that becomes impossible, extricate yourself assertively.

Chapter 3

Not making a decision is still making a choice.

When a difficult decision is looming, sometimes we choose to not make any decision. We say:

"It's too hard to decide."

It is important to recognize that *not* making a decision is still making a choice. And when we choose to *not* decide we must accept the fallout for that choice. For example, a decision needs to be made about whether an older parent should continue to drive. You choose to *not* decide whether they should or shouldn't. This means someone else might decide how that situation is going to roll out. A sibling decides Mom shouldn't be driving anymore and takes control of the situation. They tell Mom she can't drive anymore and sell Mom's car. You have chosen to *not* weigh in on the decision and, therefore, you do not get to critique the other person's choice. That said, if the decision affects you, be assertive about your participation in the outcome. For example, you get to choose how often you participate in driving Mom where she needs to go.

There can be other kinds of fallout when we choose to *not* make a decision. Someone's feelings might get hurt. While you don't "make" anyone feel a particular emotion (chapter seven in *Stop Talking to Yourself and Start Listening*), your choice to not prioritize a decision does have ramifications. Imagine that a friend has invited you to attend their event, and it is a long drive away. Rather than decide whether you feel up for the drive or not, you put off the decision. *Not* deciding sends a message that this decision is not important and that your friend and their event are not important to you—not to mention the position it puts your friend in not knowing how many people will be attending. If a decision has options, it is probably worth weighing the pros and cons and making a choice. It will just take thinking the choices through with careful consideration.

Sometimes we choose to *not* make a decision because it feels too painful—either to you or the other person. When we recognize *not* making a decision is the same as making one, we can begin to see how *not* making a decision is actually the more painful choice. Apart from the fallout pointed out in the above paragraph, indecision gnaws on us. It interrupts sleep and eating. Work becomes more difficult because we struggle to concentrate on the task at hand. We are reminded of that painful decision without even realizing it. The decision about a relationship or an elderly loved one's care might be painful or difficult to discuss. But getting it out in the open allows it to be processed and helps everyone to move on—everyone, but especially you. Once a decision is made, the new reality can take place. More decisions might be prompted by your choice but the first one is out of the way and forward motion can commence.

I am a fan of letting the universe help me make a decision. However, I fully recognize that, if I let the universe guide my decision, I can't rant at the universe later at the unfairness of it all. I have made a choice, and I need to make the best of it. Usually I realize the universe was right all along and I just need to get on board! That is the problem with *not* making a decision: you are choosing to let someone or something be in charge of your life. Is that what you want? Occasionally, I do give the decision to the universe. When I applied to graduate school, I was unsure I had what it took to successfully complete the program. I made the choice to "apply and see if they accept me and then I'll decide if I'm going or not." I chuckle at the absurdity of that sentence now. If Sage College decided I was master's degree material, of course I was going. But for some reason, I could not make the choice or say out loud, "I want to go to graduate school." But I made a choice. I chose to *apply* to graduate school. I wanted to go to graduate school. I just couldn't say it. I was making a decision without making a choice. Or I made the easier choice: to apply. Am I splitting hairs? Sure. But I believe it is an important difference. I made a decision about a decision that allowed my life to have forward motion.

Life throws difficult choices at us. Opportunities arise that come with hard choices. Painful decisions need to be made. The decisions we don't want to make are often the most important choices we need to make. It can be helpful to acknowledge the difficulty you are having making a choice. Sometimes while the dilemma is being discussed the choice becomes clear. If your decision involves someone else, begin a conversation. You might find out they are struggling as well or they may present a completely different choice that you never considered. Communication is a key factor in making choices easier. Making a choice can be hard but *not* making one is harder.

Chapter 4

There is no right or wrong choice.

I co-facilitate a therapy group at work, and we always say there is no right or wrong answer to the homework. The way the participants read the questions and respond produces the correct answers for them. The *process* is the point of the exercise. We instruct them to read the assignment, think about it and how it applies to them, and then answer. Choices should be handled the same way. There is no right or wrong choice. We each view the world through our own experiences and personality. Each choice that is presented will feel and look different to each of us.

As you "read" the world around you and the circumstances surrounding your choice, you make a decision to pursue a path. The choices you make are based on your subjective view of the world at that time. Hopefully, especially if you read my first book, *Stop Talking to Yourself and Start Listening,* you have set your boundaries, listened to yourself and view the world through your lens and not others' lenses. You know that making a decision is part of the process to pursue your life's path. Thus, no decision is right or wrong; it is just another step on your unique journey.

Sometimes, a decision ends up not being helpful or takes you off your chosen path. If this happens, you should pivot, make different choices and get back on the path you envision for yourself.

Doing this is easier if you don't waste a lot of time beating yourself up over a "bad" decision. We all make mistakes. Brush yourself off and move on. I know this is hard for some people because it used to be hard for me. In my family, traveling from point A to point B is a popular discussion. For example, every time a visitor left my parents' house, my father would ask the question, "Do you know how to get home from here?" My husband quickly realized that the best answer was an emphatic:

"Yes, sure do. Thanks!"

Otherwise, my Dad would pull out the map and a thirty-minute conversation on how to best get to the highway from their house would ensue.

Road travel is my family's thing. And we like to figure out the best way to get places. I have actually responded to the question, "How should I go to your mom's?" with the response, "Well if you go on Route 146 it's twenty-four minutes, but if you take Center Road it's 27 minutes but more pleasant." I say this as if three minutes is an important amount of time. So, imagine how I feel when I make the choice to go a certain way and realize it's longer or full of traffic jams. Back in the day, that would result in a lot of yelling and self-recrimination that usually started with, "You're so stupid."

I believe that my meditation and yoga practice—and a lot of hard work to replace negative self-talk with positive self-talk—have helped me to stop beating myself up over "poor" choices. Instead, I now move on with a philosophical, *I won't do that again!* Choices are simply one way to proceed. If the first way doesn't work, try another. My story is not going to be your story, but the message is the same: Don't waste time beating yourself up. Move on and get back on your path.

Some choices can feel life-altering. Those can be scary to make. A decision to end a relationship or change jobs, for example, can be fraught with emotion as well as practical considerations. When these choices present themselves, take your time and work through them with a trusted friend or family member. By trusted I mean someone who doesn't have an interest in your decisions or is able to separate out their needs and wants from yours. This is where it becomes important to use your boundary work. Your mom might not want you to move away no matter how awesome the job is that is being considered. If she can put aside her desires and debate the pros and cons of the job, then talk it over with her. If she can't let go of wanting you close, then she is not the person to help process this decision. Being scared is normal when you are moving on to a different path or taking on a different way of being. Feedback helps you process the choice. Move slowly. But keep moving. Your comfort level will increase as you move along the path. And if it doesn't, then you might not be moving in the right direction. Listen to yourself. You'll know if it's the right choice or not. Fear feels different from being uncomfortable with change.

Chapter 5

You can. You choose not to.

This chapter follows the previous chapter for a reason. Life-altering choices seem impossible. So, we often give up without trying, by saying:

"I can't do that."

The reality is you probably *can* do whatever is under discussion. But instead, we say, "I can't get up early and exercise," to move toward that oft-discussed weight loss or healthy living goal; "I can't switch careers," in a discussion about how much you hate your job; "I can't talk to them about that," in a conversation about someone who irritates you. The reality is you *can* do that thing you think you can't. You are choosing not to move out of your comfort zone and do it.

It is hard. Choosing to follow your passion for art as a career when your entire family is in the medical profession is hard. Choosing to get up and walk every morning when everyone else hits the snooze button until the last possible minute is hard and potentially alienating. Choosing to be successful when everyone around you chooses not to be successful is scary, hard and alienating. The good news is with the right support group and positive self-talk you can make those changes and move toward a more authentic life.

If you are trying to make changes to your life I recommend *The War of Art* by Stephen Pressfield. I found it enormously helpful when I was trying to change my life to live more authentically. In this fast-paced, easy-to-read book, Pressfield outlines what keeps us from our goals and how you can overcome those obstacles. I highly recommend it if you are struggling to make choices that move you toward your goals. For example, I pulled out the book and reread it prior to sitting down to write this book. Any time I know I am struggling to make a difficult choice, I pull out *The War of Art* and am rewarded with a renewed sense of purpose and drive to stay on my path and make the difficult choice even when it involves change.

Do you have a habit of saying:

"I can't do that"?

If so, you need to explore why. Sometimes people who say "I can't do that" a lot did not grow up empowered to accomplish things. Sometimes people who often say "I can't" had what they see as a miserable failure, and they are afraid of "failing" again. Sometimes "I can't" really means "I don't want to." The important question is "Which one of those are you?"

If you don't come from an empowering family, create one. I am a big fan of support networks. Find people who are living a life you admire and become friends with them. Spend time with the friends who do support you and stop spending as much time with those who don't. Practice your boundary work (chapter 5 in *Stop Talking to Yourself and Start Listening*), so it becomes easier when people challenge the choices you are making. Pressfield talks about this a lot in *The War of Art*. Often others' dissatisfaction with you working on your goals is about them and not you. Spend less time with those who don't nourish you and more time with people who do. Build a support network of people who want to see you accomplish your goals. It is important to recognize this work will feel uncomfortable. You will be rejecting the family message or role for yourself. That is why a strong support network is a key component to decision making. You will need support to ride out this change. Build it and your new path will be smoother.

Someone who comes from a family that didn't empower them probably engages in a lot of negative self-talk. Try to change how you talk to yourself. I work at not saying, *You're so stupid*—not because I was told I was stupid, but because it's what I heard family members say about themselves when something went wrong. When I hear myself call myself stupid, I stop and counter the argument. I say to myself, *I am not stupid. I just won't make the same mistake again – hopefully!* Pay attention to the little voice inside your head. It could be a big reason you don't reach your goals.

Maybe you messed up big time a while back and you fear messing up again. Mistakes can be painful, costly and embarrassing. Own that fear. Recognize the mistake and examine it. Did you act rashly? Did you not understand the consequences? Talk out the "mistake" with a trusted friend. Turn the "mistake" into a learning experience. Work on laughing about your learning experiences. That, in turn, empowers others to feel better about their "mistakes" and—boom!—you have just grown your support network and empowered someone else.

Whatever the reasons you say "I can't" to choices, examine those reasons and work to change them. Explore your feelings and ingrained responses. Be honest. Can you do that thing you think you can't? Or do you choose not to?

Chapter 6

Meditation

Meditation may seem like an odd choice in a book about making choices, but I believe it is a helpful tool. According to Jon Kabat-Zinn, meditation is a way to wake up and become active participants in our lives. Meditation is a practice used to increased mindfulness. When we live mindfully, we are living in the present with intention and without judgment. When we live with intention, we make choices with careful thought and consideration and an eye toward our values and goals. Developing a meditation practice will help you become mindful in your life and, in particular, about the choices that are presented to you.

So often, we rely on decision-making skills that are dependent on the needs and wants of others. We go through life without much thought—almost on autopilot—doing what is expected of us. Our decisions are made against the backdrop of judgment and anxieties. When choices crop up, even advantageous opportunities, they can feel uncomfortable and burdensome. It becomes easier to stay in the routine even if it has become a rut. If your life has begun to feel like a rut, I encourage you to open up your mind by developing a meditation practice. There are lots of great tools out there, from classes to books to apps for your phone, to learn about and grow a meditation practice.

This is another way to expand your support network. If you are new to meditation, you will meet new people who think or act in the ways you are moving towards on your new path. Or you might find current friends who have also brought meditation into their lives. Change that includes the bonus of additions to your support network is a good thing.

Meditation increases your ability to live in the moment with intention and without judgment. When we live with intention, choices become easier. If you are intentionally living your life to your own specifications, choices become clearer. Does this choice nourish me and lie within my values and goals? If you enjoy doing for others and a life of service is the life you want, then answering "yes" to helping others is an easier choice. However, sometimes your inner self would like a word with your outer self, because it is feeling overwhelmed. Some time spent meditating allows room for that inner voice to speak and be heard.

Being heard, for me, is the beauty of meditation. When I sit in stillness for even just a few minutes, I am always amazed at how much easier life becomes. Without meditation, my mind tends to move at a million miles an hour and I hop from one idea to another. I need lists to stay organized or my life feels chaotic. All that energy and movement can keep me from hearing myself. Since I began meditating, I sleep better and am less annoyed throughout my day. I hear myself when I need to take a break or choose a slower pace. I also accomplish more important items on my to-do list rather than just a lot of busy work.

Meditation is a choice and it might not be for you. If you have been curious about it, I encourage you to give it a try. It can be as involved as joining a meditation group to as simple as sitting and focusing on your breath for two minutes a few times a day. It is called a meditation practice for a reason, though. It takes practice to be able to sit in stillness without judgment. Try not to become discouraged if it is difficult at first. Sometimes the things that are most difficult at first provide the biggest rewards.

Chapter 7

Simplify

Simplify. It's become a buzzword these days. But how does simplifying your life relate to making choices? When you begin to simplify your life, you start by getting rid of those things that don't fulfill you, match your goals or values, and add clutter and no real value to your life. Simplifying will make choices easier to decide.

Simplifying is a great way to start getting an idea of what is important to you. For example, you start cleaning out your closet and discover you have a loved and large collection of outdoor exercise wear. It dawns on you that you have not been making getting outside and exercising a priority. Life got in the way, you say. But it's your life and these are your life choices. The simplifying of your closet has shone a light on some new choices you need to start making. The same thing can be said for a bookcase. The majority of the books are travel books, but you haven't chosen to take a trip in a long time. Maybe it's time to choose to start a travel fund and plan a trip.

If your time seems to move along at a frantic pace, it is time to simplify your activities. If you're a parent, the place to start simplifying is your child's activities. When we are just filling time, it is important to look at why. It is more important to help our children find a passion than to just fill their days with activities so they won't find something "bad" to do. If you're the person who is filling time rather than intentionally spending time doing chosen things, it's time to ask why. Mindless activity creates the illusion of a happy, fulfilled life. Try to intentionally plan your time to match your values and goals. You may need to start with small changes, but it is your intention that is important—quality over quantity.

What is the difference between alone and lonely? People can be alone and very content. People can be with a crowd of friends and feel lonely. Our living spaces are the same way. Have you ever walked into someone's home and thought that the home was beautiful but also very cold? There are lovely things but no warmth. Do you ever look around your own living space and feel like it doesn't represent you? Or it overwhelms you? It is time to simplify your living space.

A number of years ago, we downsized houses. We wanted more money for experiences and less stuff. We wanted more time for fun and less time spent on yard and housework. It worked. By simplifying our home space, we freed up time, energy, and money to make more authentic choices. That was our choice. We are friends with a couple who bought an old home that they are restoring. They spend their weekends fixing up their old house that they love. That was their choice. They still get out on the water paddling with us occasionally, but they are choosing to spend the bulk of their free time bringing their old home back to life.

What you spend your time doing is your choice. But if your life is so cluttered with things and activities that you can't see your way through, then it is time to simplify. Your passions are probably hidden under all that clutter. Start de-cluttering and find your passions. Then make choices that honor those passions.

Chapter 8

Fine, I'll decide. But how?

There you are living your life and along comes a decision you don't really want to make. Maybe it is a big one: you have to decide if your marriage is working for you. Or, your elderly parent exhibits poor life management skills and you have to decide if they can live alone anymore. Maybe it's good news: your company just opened an office in your dream city and there is a position there for you if you want it. Even good change can be stressful. The choices are stressful, and I believe it is important to acknowledge the stress. Acknowledging something takes away some of its power and moves you forward toward a decision.

Difficult choices come with difficult questions. It helps to have a support network of people that you can discuss things with. Sometimes just talking about a subject makes it less scary or painful, and the decision becomes easier to manage. Talking to someone who has experience dealing with elderly parents may provide you with, not only a sympathetic ear, but also, options you weren't aware of. Knowledge is power. Finding someone who knows the city you are considering moving to is a step toward gathering information that will help you formulate your decision.

Sometimes our support network has a vested interest in our decisions. Normally, you may talk to family members about your career, but, if a career move means you will have to move away from them, then they may not be your best option for an initial discussion about your decision. Find someone who doesn't have a major stake in your decision but still knows you well enough to provide relevant feedback.

Once you have talked to people who know you and/or the situation begin writing down your different choices. Sometimes writing more is better, and sometimes it makes the situation feel even more daunting. However, it can help you to have a realistic, full picture of your situation. In the writing of your options, your choice may jump out at you. Then all you need to do is make that decision. However, sometimes in the writing of the possible options, it becomes obvious there is more than one option that could work.

One tool I use for those decisions—big or small—is a pros and cons worksheet, which is simple and straightforward. I have included an example on the following page.

Decision:

Pros	Cons

This exercise is pretty elementary. Choose one of the decisions, and then write down all the pros for that decision. Next, write down all the cons. For example, if you are trying to decide whether to stay in your marriage, you could put together a pros and cons list. Your pros may include financial comfort and a shared love of traveling. Your cons may include feeling disrespected and an overall daily dissatisfaction with life.

Once you get your pros and cons down on paper, your decision might be clearer to see. Or you might realize there are some things you could assertively address. Something I say to my clients frequently is that the only person you control is you. For example, you can't change another person's disrespectful treatment of you, but you can change how you respond to it. You can change your daily dissatisfaction with life by changing those parts of your daily life that you do control. Your pros list might be really short and the cons list really long and, in that case, the decision to leave might become: not if, but when. Conversely, your pros list might be longer than you realized—and your cons list really short. You might remember all those things you had forgotten you enjoyed doing with your partner. Then, the decision to stay would likely become the clear winner. I like the pros and cons sheet because it is a concrete, unemotional way to look at a decision that may have become complicated by your emotions and frustration.

For those less emotional decisions, like a job offer that does not involve moving or a vacation locale, it is still a good idea to get your thoughts down on paper. I think back to long, painful discussions with my spouse about choosing a vacation locale and accommodations, and I wish we had used this tool. One year, we got so mired in our own needs and wants that we gave up and didn't go on vacation! If we had just put our discussion down on paper, we might have been able to work past our emotions, examine the pros and cons in a concrete way, and make a choice—and we would have actually gone on vacation!

For a discussion involving things like vacations or house hunting, I suggest a needs and wants worksheet. In that scenario, each person gets a worksheet and lists their needs and wants for that decision. For example, the decision is where to go on vacation. Each person writes down what they need and want from the vacation. My needs would include walkability, privacy, nearby restaurants and a body of water. My wants would include air conditioning and staying at a place within an eight-hour car ride because I don't like to fly. It's in the want column because I would prefer to drive but would fly for a great locale. Then my spouse and I could compare our worksheets and see what matches up. Since my husband enjoys being in the middle of the action, assertive negotiation would need to take place. Privacy is a vague concept. If the accommodation is in the middle of town but offers a private terrace, I would consider it—whereas, for my spouse, a beach house on a dead-end street would be too far removed from the action.

Getting those needs and wants down on paper allows for a more detailed discussion with less chance of misunderstandings. This exercise allows for a less emotional discussion because both parties are able to think about—and take note of—their personal needs and wants. Then, they should be able to negotiate to a compromise. I have included a needs and wants sheet on the following page.

Decision:

Needs	Wants

Conclusion

Making decisions is hard work. The rewards of a well-thought-out decision are huge. Take the time to understand what is important to you. Work on creating strong boundaries. Create a life that honors your passions and values. Your decisions, both everyday and life-changing ones, will become easier to manage and make.

References

Kabat-Zinn, Jon (1994). *Wherever You Go, There You Are: Mindfulness Meditation in Everyday Life.* New York, NY: Hyperion.

Pressfield, Steven. (2002). *The War of Art: Break Through the Blocks and Win Your Inner Creative Battles.*

www.ingramcontent.com/pod-product-compliance
Lightning Source LLC
Chambersburg PA
CBHW020444090526
44586CB00045B/838